Transformations in Nature

A Seed Becomes a Dandelion

Amy Hayes

Cavendish Square
New York

Published in 2016 by Cavendish Square Publishing, LLC
243 5th Avenue, Suite 136, New York, NY 10016

First Edition

Website: cavendishsq.com

This publication represents the opinions and views of the author based on his or her personal experience, knowledge, and research. The information in this book serves as a general guide only. The author and publisher have used their best efforts in preparing this book and disclaim liability rising directly or indirectly from the use and application of this book.

CPSIA Compliance Information: Batch #CW16CSQ

All websites were available and accurate when this book was sent to press.

Library of Congress Cataloging-in-Publication Data

Hayes, Amy, author.
A seed becomes a dandelion / Amy Hayes.
pages cm. — (Transformations in nature)
Includes index.
ISBN 978-1-5026-0828-4 (hardcover) ISBN 978-1-5026-0826-0 (paperback) ISBN 978-1-5026-0829-1 (ebook)
1. Common dandelion—Juvenile literature. 2. Seeds—Juvenile literature. I. Title.
QK495.C74H39 2016
583'.99—dc23
2015023861

Editorial Director: David McNamara
Copy Editor: Rebecca Rohan
Art Director: Jeffrey Talbot
Designer: Stephanie Flecha
Senior Production Manager: Jennifer Ryder-Talbot
Production Editor: Renni Johnson
Photo Research: J8 Media

The photographs in this book are used by permission and through the courtesy of: Zadiraka Evgenii/Shutterstock.com, Konstanttin/Shutterstock.com, cover; Hakan Jansson/Maskot/Getty Images, 5; Wally Eberhart/Visuals Unlimited/Getty Images, 7; Johner Images/Johner Images Royalty-Free/Getty Images, 9; Elizabeth/Flickr Flash/Getty Images, 11; Maria Rafaela Schulze-Vorberg/Moment Open/Getty Images, 13; Annika hlander/EyeEm/Getty Images, 15; Janis Litavnieks/E+/Getty Images, 19; gabyrusu/Shutterstock.com, 21.

Printed in the United States of America

Contents

Dandelions come from **seeds**.

5

First, a **root** grows
out from the seed.

7

After that, **shoots** with leaves grow.

9

A **stem** grows out
from the ground.

11

The stem has a bud.

13

The bud becomes
a bright yellow **flower**.

15

A bee lands on the flower.

17

The petals fall off.
Seeds grow.

19

The seeds blow away to grow more dandelions.

21

New Words

flower (FLOW-er) The colorful leaves of a plant where fruit and seeds are made.

root (ROOT) Part of the plant that grows underground.

seeds (SEEDZ) Small parts of a plant that can turn into new plants.

shoot (SHOOT) Part of a new plant that is just beginning to grow.

stem (STEM) A part of a plant that supports leaves, flowers, or fruit.

22

Index

About the Author

Amy Hayes lives in the beautiful city of Buffalo, New York. She has written several books for children, including *Hornets, Medusa and Pegasus, From Wax to Crayons*, and *We Need Worms!*

About BOOK WORMS

Bookworms help independent readers gain reading confidence through high-frequency words, simple sentences, and strong picture/text support. Each book explores a concept that helps children relate what they read to the world they live in.